Understanding the Human Body

Muscles and the Skeleton

Robert Snedden

WAYLAND

First published in 2009 by Wayland
338 Euston Road
London NW1 3BH

Wayland Australia
Level 17/207 Kent Street
Sydney NSW 2000

British Library Cataloguing in Publication Data
Snedden, Robert
    Muscles and skeleton. - (Understanding the human body)
    1. Musculoskeletal system - Juvenile literature
    I. Title
    612.7

    ISBN: 978 0 7502 5728 2

Produced for Wayland by Discovery Books Limited
Managing Editor: Laura Durman
Editor: Kathryn Walker
Wayland editor: Katie Powell
Design and illustrations: sprout.uk.com
Picture research: Rachel Tisdale
Series consultant: Sue Hyem

Printed in China

Wayland is a division of Hachette Children's Books,
an Hachette UK Company
www.hachette.co.uk

Photo acknowledgements: Discovery Picture Library: p. 31 (Laura
Durman); Getty Images: p. 7 (Imagno); Istockphoto.com: cover
(Eric Hood Photography), pp. 16, 20 (Alan Crawford), p. 22 (Laurent
Nicolaon); Science Photo Library: p. 11 (Steve Gschmeissner), p. 17
(Prof. P. Motta/Dept. of Anatomy/University 'La Sapienza', Rome),
p. 26 (Steve Gschmeissner), p. 34 (Steve Gschmeissner), p. 36
(D. Phillips); Shutterstock: title page & p. 18 (Salamanderman), p. 6
(Monkey Business Images), p. 9 (Geir Olav Lyngfjell), p. 13 (Matthew
Jacques), p. 15 (Michael Svoboda), p. 23 (Peter Elvidge), p. 24 (Anna
Dzondzua), p. 25 (Losersky Pavel), p. 29 (Felix Mizionikov), p. 32
(Lorelyn Medina), p. 35 (Benis Arapovic), p. 38 (Orange Line Media),
p. 39 (Pete Saloutos), p. 40 (Bartlomiej K. Kwieciszewski), p. 41
(John A. Anderson), p. 42 (Gabriel Moisa), p. 43 (Mateus Kopyt).

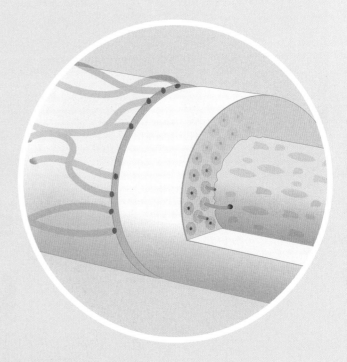

Contents

The shape I'm in

Have you ever wondered why your body is the shape it is? The size of your skeleton and your muscular development are two of the main factors in giving you your shape. This book will look at the human skeleton and muscular system, not only at how our bones and muscles give us shape, but how they work together to give us movement and protect our internal organs.

Body building

A person's height is determined by the size of their skeleton, and there isn't much that anyone can do to change that. The length of the longest bones in the body, the tibia and fibula in the lower leg and the femur, or thigh bone, will largely determine how tall someone is. Generally, these bones will have reached their full length by about age 17 and there are no exercises or diets that will make them grow any longer.

Everyone has a different body shape, and people's heights vary depending on the size of their skeletons.

Muscles add shape to the bare bones of your skeleton, and we can add or lose muscle by exercise (or lack of it). Regular exercise will strengthen and bulk out muscles, as well as increase your stamina and overall fitness. Between a third and a half of your body weight will be made up of muscle. Together, your skeleton and your muscles provide the framework and protection for the rest of your body.

On the move

Of course, your skeleton and muscles do a lot more than just provide somewhere to house your other body parts. They are the means by which we move around. If your skeleton was a rigid frame you wouldn't be able to move at all, but the bones are joined together at joints. There are joints in your arms, your legs, your fingers and toes and along your backbone, all giving you the flexibility to move.

Moving doesn't just need joints – it needs muscles to provide the power to move those joints. The body's major muscles are attached to bones. When these muscles contract, they pull on the bones, moving them around the joints.

More muscles

The muscles that you use to move around are called skeletal muscles. But they aren't the only type of muscle in your body. A different type of muscle, called smooth muscle, takes care of things that go on without you thinking about them, such as the movement of food through the digestive system. There is also a third kind of muscle. This is called cardiac muscle and it keeps your heart beating.

Body facts

The tallest man who ever lived was Robert Pershing Wadlow of Illinois, USA, who stood 2.72 metres (8 feet 11 inches) tall. His arm span was 2.88 m (9 ft 5 in) and his hands measured 32.4 centimetres (12.8 in) from wrist to middle fingertip. Wadlow died in July 1940, aged 22.

Robert Pershing Wadlow, the tallest man who ever lived, is pictured here with his brothers on his 17th birthday.

The skeleton

The skeleton is the body's internal framework, supporting the softer parts that surround it and protecting some internal organs. If somehow your skeleton were to be removed from your body, you would collapse in an unattractive heap!

Big bones, little bones

There are 206 bones in the adult human body. Children start out with more bones – about 300 – but as they grow some of these fuse together. Each bone has a distinctive role to play in the body, ranging from the bones of the spine that allow you to stand up straight, to the tiny auditory ossicles in the ear that are essential for hearing, the long load-bearing bones of the thighs and the tough skull that protects the brain.

Strong bones

Bones are incredibly tough – they have to be to absorb all the demands of an active human – and yet very light, too. They can withstand stretching forces that would crack concrete.

Try this

Take some clean chicken bones and put them in a container with enough vinegar to cover them. Leave them in the vinegar for a day or two. When you take them out of the vinegar they should be soft enough to tie in knots. What happens is that the vinegar dissolves the calcium salts in the bone. Without the calcium, the bone loses its rigidity.

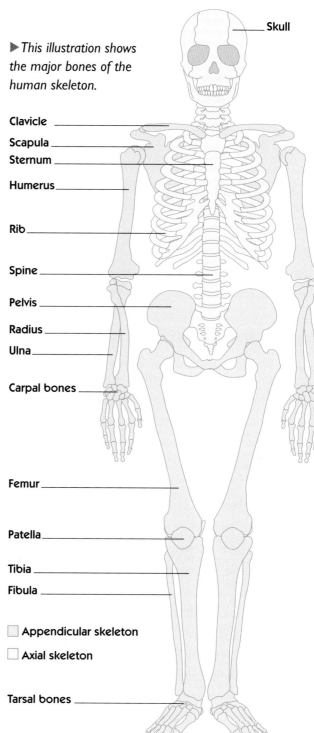

► This illustration shows the major bones of the human skeleton.

Skull

Clavicle

Scapula

Sternum

Humerus

Rib

Spine

Pelvis

Radius

Ulna

Carpal bones

Femur

Patella

Tibia

Fibula

☐ Appendicular skeleton

☐ Axial skeleton

Tarsal bones

The skeleton is strong and tough enough to withstand the stresses of energetic activities. But for activities that carry the risk of head injury, it is important to wear helmets that help protect the skull and brain.

If your skeleton was made of steel that is as strong as your bones are, it would be five times heavier than it actually is. The lightness and strength of your skeleton comes from the combination of strong materials that make up bones (page 10-11) and also from the structure of a bone – particularly the long bones. They are like long tubes with a hollow centre, and, weight for weight, a tube is stronger than a solid rod.

Two skeletons in one

The bones of the body are divided into two groups. The axial skeleton is the central part of the body, including the skull, the spine, the ribs and the sternum (breastbone). It provides the anchor for the rest of the body, which is called the appendicular skeleton. This consists of the shoulders, arms, hands and fingers, together with the hips, legs, feet and toes.

Body facts

The longest bone in the body is the femur, or thigh bone. It can be over a quarter of an adult's total height.

The smallest bone is the stapes, one of the auditory ossicles, at 2.5 – 3.5 millimetres (0.1 – 0.14 in) long.

In a 65-kilogram (143-lb) adult, the skeleton will weigh about 9 kg (20 lbs).

The bones of the body are linked together by over 230 joints.

Living bones

Looking at a skeleton, it is easy to think of bones as dead, but in a living body this is very far from the truth. Your bones are just as much alive as any other part of your body. Bones contain blood vessels, nerve cells and living bone cells held together in a framework of hard, non-living material produced and maintained by the bone cells.

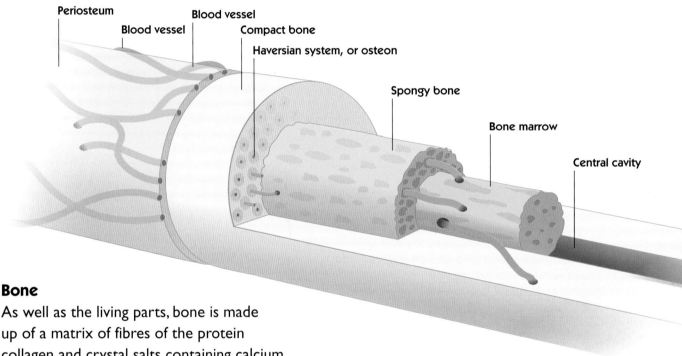

Periosteum
Blood vessel
Blood vessel
Compact bone
Haversian system, or osteon
Spongy bone
Bone marrow
Central cavity

Bone

As well as the living parts, bone is made up of a matrix of fibres of the protein collagen and crystal salts containing calcium and other minerals. Collagen and calcium help to strengthen bones. The collagen resists stretching forces and the calcium resists compression forces. Bones are in some ways similar in construction to reinforced concrete – the collagen fibres are like the steel rods in the concrete, while the calcium salts are like the cement and sand between them.

Compact bone

There are two types of bone tissue: compact bone and spongy bone. Four-fifths of the skeleton is made up of compact bone.

▲ *This illustration shows a simplified cross-section through one of the body's long bones.*

The outer shells of all bones and the shafts of the long limb bones are made of compact bone.

Compact bone consists of many closely packed rod-like units called Haversian systems, or osteons. A central canal, or channel, runs down the centre of each of these rods carrying blood vessels and nerve fibres.

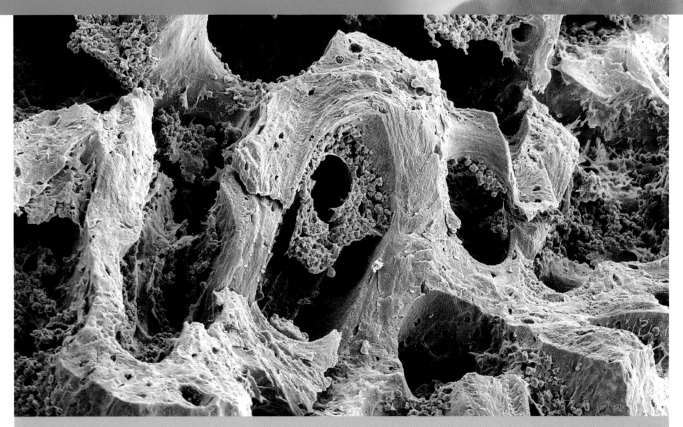

This greatly magnified image shows bone marrow inside spongy bone tissue.

Concentric rings called lamellae surround the canal. Within these rings there are dark spots where osteocytes, a type of bone cell, are found. Small channels connect these dark spots to the central canal, providing passageways for nutrients to reach the bone cells through the hard surrounding material.

A thin membrane called the periosteum covers the surface of the bones. This is rich with blood vessels bringing nutrients to the bone. The blood vessels in the canals interconnect with the vessels on the surface of the bone.

Spongy bone

Spongy bone is the tissue that makes up the interior of bones. It is lighter and less dense than compact bone. Spongy bone consists of thin plates and bars of bone just a few cells thick next to small, irregular cavities that contain red bone marrow (see below). There is no central canal. The plates and bars of the spongy bone are organised to provide maximum strength combined with lightness.

Bone marrow

As well as filling the spaces in spongy bone, bone marrow is also found in the central cavity that runs along the centre of long bones, such as the femur. Bone marrow is jelly-like in appearance. It is a very important part of the body because it is here that blood cells are formed. Both red blood cells, which carry oxygen to all parts of the body, and white blood cells, which are part of the body's defences against infection, grow from cells in the bone marrow.

Growing bones

As you grow from infancy to adulthood, your skeleton is constantly becoming bigger and stronger. The long bones, such as those in your arms and legs, get steadily longer and thicker and you take on the proportions of an adult. A baby's head is relatively large, but the growth of the head slows as the growth of the limbs and body speed up. Most of your bones will be fully developed by the time you are about 20 years old.

The infant skeleton

In the womb the foetus (unborn baby) has no hard skeleton to begin with as the skeleton develops first as a hard, bendy tissue called cartilage (see page 16). Gradually the cartilage is replaced by bone and by birth all of the bones will have formed. This process of bonemaking is called ossification.

A newborn baby has more bones than an adult, with pockets of cartilage between bones that allows further growth to take place. The number of bones is reduced as some, such as the bones that make up the skull and the pelvis, fuse together.

The fontanelles are soft areas on a baby's skull where the bones have not yet fused together. They allow the baby's head to be squeezed slightly as it is being born. The fontanelles close up by around 18 months after birth.

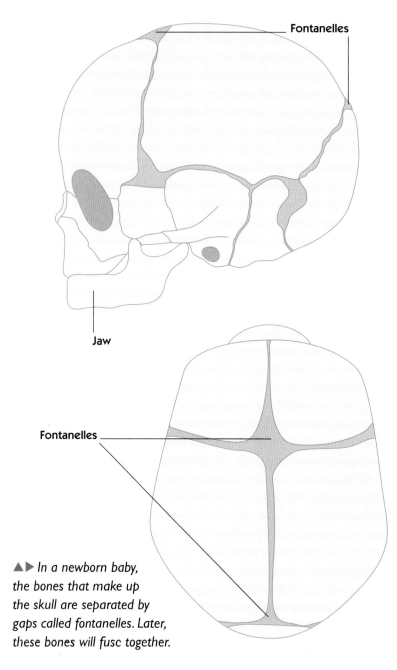

Fontanelles

Jaw

Fontanelles

▲▶ *In a newborn baby, the bones that make up the skull are separated by gaps called fontanelles. Later, these bones will fuse together.*

How bones grow in length

As you grow into an adult, your limbs grow in length. A long bone, such as your femur (thigh bone), grows in length at either end in regions called growth plates.

Growth occurs when cartilage cells in these growth plates divide and increase in number. The new cartilage cells push older, larger cartilage cells towards the middle of the bone.

When a bone has reached its full size, its growth plates are converted from cartilage into bone. Long bone growth stops at the end of puberty. Puberty is the process of body changes that takes place during adolescence. When long bone growth stops, you stop getting taller.

Other bones, such as those in the ankles and wrists, will continue to thicken and grow stronger up to the age of about 20.

Body facts

There are some animals that even in adulthood have skeletons that are made entirely of cartilage. They include sharks and rays, creatures that live in a watery environment where their skeletons don't have to support their weight and where flexibility is an advantage.

Your height is mostly determined by the length of your bones, particularly your leg bones. For these basketball players, having long bones is an advantage!

Bone shapes

The various bones in the human body can be grouped according to their shape. For example, long bones, as the name suggests, are much longer than they are wide. Most of the limb bones and finger bones are long bones. Short bones are roughly as wide as they are long and block-shaped. They include the carpal bones of the wrist and the tarsal bones of the foot.

Long bones

Long bones are the bones involved in making big movements, like swinging your arms and walking. They are long and cylindrical in shape.

The bone ends are covered by tough, smooth cartilage. Bone growth takes place in the growth plates that lie between the head of the bone and the shaft. Examples of long bones include the femur (thigh bone), the humerus (the upper bone in the arm) and the phalanges (fingers and toes).

Short bones

Short bones are almost cube shaped and are associated with more complex and delicate movements than the long bones, such as flexing and rotating the wrist.

Short bones have no central shaft and have a hard outer shell of compact bone around a centre of spongy bone. Examples of short bones include the carpal bones (small bones in the base of the hand) and tarsal bones (found in the feet).

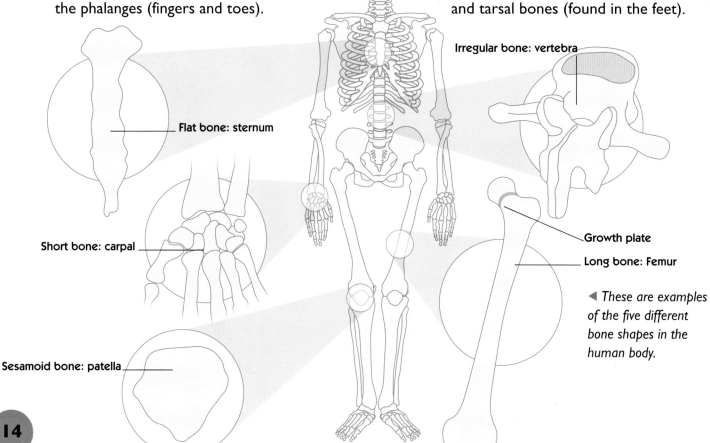

Flat bone: sternum

Irregular bone: vertebra

Short bone: carpal

Growth plate

Long bone: Femur

Sesamoid bone: patella

◄ *These are examples of the five different bone shapes in the human body.*

14

The long bones of the arms and legs are involved in big movements like swinging your arms and jumping.

Flat bones

Flat bones are actually curved, not flat – most of the bones in the skull, the sternum (breastbone) and the scapulas (shoulder blades) are flat bones. They are made up of a layer of spongy bone sandwiched between two layers of compact bone.

Flat bones, like the skull bones, can give protection to internal organs or they can provide a large area to which muscles are attached. For example, a number of muscles involved in moving the arm are attached to the shoulder blade, which is a flat bone.

Irregular bones

Irregular bones are odd-shaped bones that don't easily fit into any of the three categories above. They include the vertebrae of the spine and the hip bones. Like the short bones, they are composed of a layer of compact bone around a centre of spongy bone.

Sesamoid bones

The sesamoid bones, are found inside tendons, where they help in joint movement and protect the tendon. Sesamoid bones are usually located over a joint, such as the knee. The patella, or knee bone, is the largest sesamoid bone in the body.

Cartilage

Your skeleton isn't entirely made from bone. Some parts of it are formed from a type of tissue called cartilage. Cartilage isn't as hard or as rigid as bone, but it is strong and tough. It is more elastic than bone, can be compressed and will bend slightly. There are different types of cartilage, such as fibrocartilage, hyaline cartilage and elastic cartilage.

What cartilage does

Cartilage has a number of roles to play in the body. For example, it acts as a shock absorber between the vertebrae of the spine so they don't crash together every time you run or jump. It covers the surface of joints and provides a smooth surface that allows bones to slide over one another, reducing friction and preventing wear and tear on the bones. Cartilage also provides additional support for the body as you move.

Cartilage acts as a mould for some parts of the body. The shape of your nose is formed by a number of curved plates of cartilage, with another cartilage plate providing the separation between your nostrils. The framework for your outer ears is also made up of cartilage.

Embedded in the cartilage are the specialised cells that build and maintain it, held within tough fibres of collagen. Unlike bone, cartilage is not supplied by blood vessels and has no nerves inside it. Damaged cartilage heals much more slowly than other tissues, such as muscles and bone.

Elastic cartilage

Elastic cartilage is the springiest and most flexible of the types of cartilage. This is the

The cartilage that makes up your ears gives them shape and flexibility.

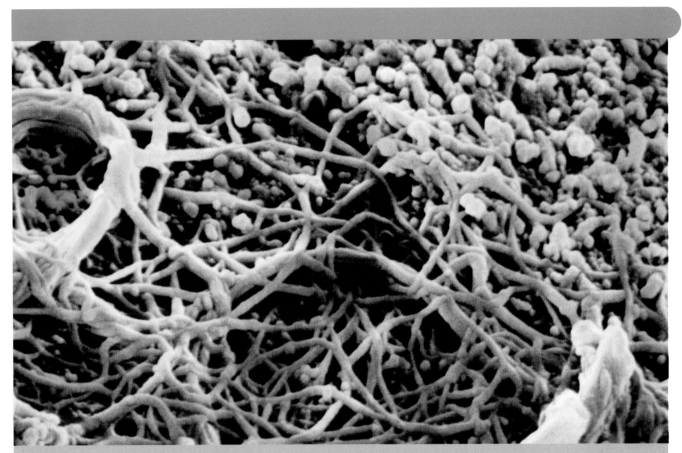

High magnification reveals the fibres that make up cartilage. This is hyaline cartilage, the sort found on the ends of long bones.

cartilage that makes up the outside of your ears, some of your nose, and also your epiglottis (the flap of tissue at the back of your throat that keeps food out of your windpipe when you swallow).

Fibrocartilage

Fibrocartilage is the toughest type of cartilage, and it is able to withstand a great deal of weight. It is also a very hard-wearing material. Fibrocartilage is found between the vertebrae of your spine and between the bones in your hips and pelvis.

Hyaline cartilage

Hyaline cartilage is both springy and tough. It is hyaline cartilage that divides your nose in two. It is between your ribs, around your windpipe, in your larynx (voice box), and in your bronchi (the tubes that carry air into your lungs).

Hyaline cartilage is also found between your joints. It covers the ends of many bones where they meet and form joints with other bones, such as at the elbow. The hyaline cartilage between your joints is known as articular cartilage.

Joints

The bones of your skeleton are not all joined tightly together –
if they were you wouldn't be able to move. Most of the bones
of your body are linked together by joints. There are three basic
types of joint: cartilaginous, fibrous and synovial.

Cartilaginous and fibrous joints

In cartilaginous joints the bones are joined by
cartilage that is flexible enough to allow them to
move slightly. Your ribs and sternum (breastbone)
are linked by cartilaginous joints. There are also
cartilaginous joints linking the vertebrae of
your spine, allowing you to bend your back.

Fibrous joints link bones rigidly, with tough
fibres that prevent any movement at all.
The joints that hold the bones of your skull
together are fibrous joints.

Synovial joints

Most of your joints are synovial joints. They allow
a much greater range of movements. The ends
of the bones are covered by smooth cartilage
and a fluid, called synovial fluid, lubricates the
joints. Tough straps of tissue called ligaments
stop the bones from moving too far apart.

There are different types of synovial joint:

Ball and socket joints, such
as the hip and shoulder joints,
allow the greatest range of
movements. The ball-shaped
end of a long bone fits inside
the socket of another bone.
These joints allow you to
swing your arms and legs in
different directions.

Without joints, our bodies would be rigid and inflexible.

Body facts

The hyoid bone in the neck is the only bone in the body that is not connected by a joint to any other bone. It sits above the larynx (voice box), held in place by strong ligaments that attach it to the skull. Only the human hyoid bone is in just the right position to work together with the larynx and tongue to produce speech. The hyoid bone helps to support the tongue and raise the larynx when you talk or swallow.

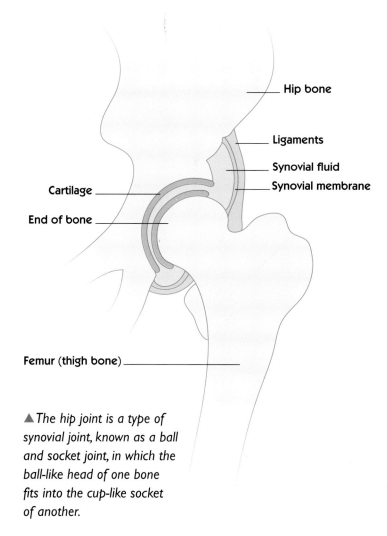

Hip bone

Ligaments

Synovial fluid

Synovial membrane

Cartilage

End of bone

Femur (thigh bone)

▲ The hip joint is a type of synovial joint, known as a ball and socket joint, in which the ball-like head of one bone fits into the cup-like socket of another.

Hinge joints allow movement that is similar to the opening and closing of a hinged door. The curved surface of one bone fits around the similar curves of another bone. These are the joints in the elbow and knees.

Ellipsoidal joints, such as the joints in the wrist, allow bending and extending, rocking from side to side, and a small amount of rotation.

Gliding joints occur between the surfaces of two flat bones that are held together by ligaments. Some of the bones in your wrists and ankles are linked by gliding joints.

Pivot joints allow bones to move around other bones, such as the joint in your neck that allows you to turn your head from side to side.

Saddle joints have bones that can rock back and forth and from side to side and allow a small amount of rotation. The only saddle joints in your body are in your thumbs.

Bone mending

Bones are tough and hard wearing but they can still be damaged. An accident can cause a bone to be cracked or even broken. When this happens, the living bone will begin the lengthy process of repairing itself.

Fractures

A broken bone is said to be fractured. There are several kinds of fracture.

Simple (or closed) fracture The bone may be cracked or snapped cleanly, but it does not protrude through the skin.

Compound fracture The bone end does break through the skin. This is more serious than a simple fracture as infection can enter through the open wound.

Greenstick fracture is one in which the bone does not break in two but cracks on one side. These fractures are most common in the supple bones of children.

Comminuted fracture is one in which the bone is crushed or splintered and may be shattered into many small pieces.

Impacted fracture results from a force pushing along the length of a bone and crushing it into another bone. A bad fall can cause this.

The healing process

The body will begin healing a broken bone right away. But any broken bone, particularly a serious injury such as a comminuted fracture, should be given proper medical attention right away to make sure that it heals properly.

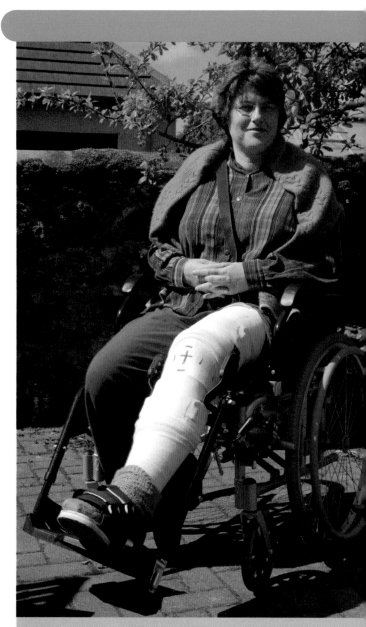

Doctors prevent a broken limb from moving with a hard cast to ensure that the bones can heal properly.

A simple fracture takes six to eight weeks to heal. First, blood vessels that have been ruptured at the break in the bone cause a swelling called a haematoma to form. The broken blood vessels are repaired by the body and begin transporting nutrients into the damaged area, keeping the bone cells alive.

After a few days, the haematoma develops into tougher fibrous tissue called a soft callus. This happens as cells called fibroblasts begin to produce strands of collagen. Another group of cells, called chondroblasts, produce cartilage which bridges the gap between the broken ends of the bone. The soft callus generally lasts about three weeks.

Finally, osteoblasts begin to produce new bone cells, turning the cartilage into a bone callus. The body begins to break down and reabsorb

Investigate

How do doctors go about helping the natural healing process of bones? One of the most important things a doctor can do is to make sure that the broken parts of the bone are aligned properly so that the bone doesn't heal in a misshapen way. Find out about all the different methods that doctors use for holding broken bones in position while they heal.

bits of dead bone, and to close the gap between the broken pieces of bone. Over a period of months, the bone callus is replaced with harder compact bone and gradually the bone is returned to its original shape.

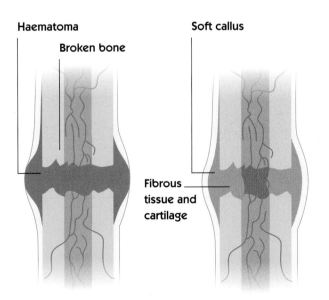

Haematoma
Broken bone

Soft callus

Fibrous tissue and cartilage

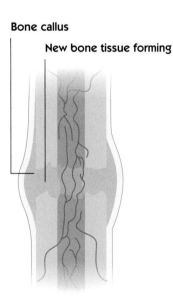

Bone callus
New bone tissue forming

New bone formation

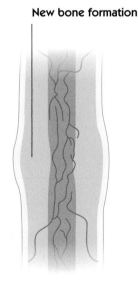

▲ 1) A swelling called a haematoma forms around the broken bone.

▲ 2) Fibrous tissue and cartilage forms a soft callus around the break area.

▲ 3) The cartilage turns into a bone callus.

▲ 4) The bone callus is replaced with new bone tissue.

Old bones

Calcium is one of the most important minerals used by the body. It is involved in muscle and nerve activity and in regulating blood pressure amongst other things. Your body uses the skeleton like a calcium bank, depositing calcium in the bones for storage and retrieving it as needed. It is important to make sure you have a good supply of calcium, particularly at a young age.

Bone mass

Your bones are being maintained all the time by your body. Up until the age of around 30 to 35, the formation of new bone mass in the body – the deposits in your calcium bank – takes place at a faster rate than old bone material is broken down. The result is that the amount of bone mass increases until it reaches a peak at about this time.

After the the age of about 30 to 35, old bone tissue is broken down faster than new bone is

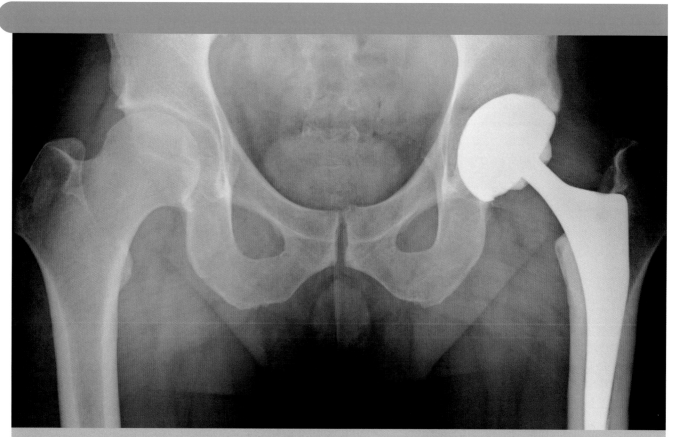

This x-ray shows an artificial hip. Replacing a worn out hip joint with an artificial one is a common operation.

produced and bone mass gradually decreases with age. The amount of calcium in the bone also decreases.

In women, bone loss is faster in the first five years after the menopause. This is because production of the hormone oestrogen, which influences bone formation, ceases after the menopause.

Osteoporosis

If large amounts of bone tissue are lost, the bones can become weak, brittle and liable to break easily. This condition is called osteoporosis. All bones can be affected by osteoporosis, but fractures are most common in the wrist, spine and hip. Fractures to the spine are what cause the hunched appearance of some older people. As well as affecting older people, osteoporosis can affect younger men and women, such as those who have suffered with eating disorders.

Arthritis

In a person suffering from the condition called arthritis, the joints become inflamed and painful. There are different types of arthritis, one of which is rheumatoid arthritis. This is a condition in which the body's own defence mechanisms 'misfire' and attack tissues in the joints.

Osteoarthritis is caused by wear and tear on the cartilage in a joint, making the joints painful to move. Osteoarthritis particularly affects major joints such as the hip. Sometimes the condition can make moving so difficult that the only solution is to replace the damaged hip with an artificial one.

Investigate

There are around 200 different types of arthritis. It is a condition that affects many people, and not just the elderly. One child in every thousand may suffer from some form of arthritis. See what you can find out about how arthritis is treated and how exercise, medicine, surgery and diet can all play a part in controlling it.

A loss of bone mass, particularly in the spine, can give older people a stooped appearance.

Healthy bones

Bone, as we have seen, is living tissue. Like the other tissues in the body, we need to keep our bones healthy by supplying their needs through a good diet. The minerals magnesium, zinc and fluoride are all needed for good bone development, but the most important is calcium. This is the most abundant mineral in bone.

Calcium

Throughout childhood, adolescence and early adulthood, large amounts of calcium and other substances are being added to the bone as the skeleton develops and strengthens. The body is not able to make calcium itself. This means that all your calcium needs must come from your diet.

The amount of calcium you need rises steadily from about 210 milligrams a day at 6 months old to 1,300 mg a day between 14 and 18 years old. After that, when most bone growth is completed, the amount needed declines. Good sources of calcium include dairy products like milk and cheese, dark green leafy vegetables and nuts, such as almonds.

Calcium is an essential part of the diet to ensure healthy bone development.

Body facts

Vitamin D is important for healthy bones because it helps the body to absorb calcium. Vitamin D is made by the action of sunlight on the skin and about 90 per cent of your body's vitamin D needs are met in this way. A deficiency of vitamin D can result in rickets. This is a condition where the sufferer feels pains in the bones, and joints may become enlarged.

Bones and genes

A lot of the differences in the ways people's bones develop is down to genetics – the characteristics you inherit from your parents. For example, over half of the variation in bone mass between individuals is down to differences in their genes. Genetic differences also explain why one person may be more likely to fracture a bone in an accident than another person.

Bones and exercise

Regular exercise isn't only good for developing your muscles, it is also good for keeping your bones healthy. Bone formation and the replacement of old bone tissue take place throughout life. These processes are influenced by a number of factors that include physical activity as well as diet.

Regular exercise such as jogging, brisk walking or dancing, particularly during childhood and adolescence, helps to strengthen developing

Regular exercise is important for building bone strength.

bones. This is because exercise encourages bone-building and so increases your peak bone mass. Being physically active throughout life is important to keep bones strong. Having strong bones in youth reduces the chances of developing osteoporosis in later life.

Connective tissue

As the name suggests, connective tissue connects other tissues in the body. Connective tissue provides support and protection and holds all of the other parts of the body together. There are many types of connective tissue. They include cartilage, the tendons that attach muscles to bone, and the ligaments that hold bones together at joints. Bone itself is actually a form of connective tissue.

Ligaments

Ligaments are made up of strands of collagen, the protein that is also found in cartilage. A network of ligaments holds together the bones in joints such as the knee and ankle. Ligaments are slightly elastic and curve gently; they can be straightened by the pull of muscles and then spring back into position when released.

Tendons

Tendons connect muscles to the bones that they pull. Sheets of tendon and ligament tissue act as anchor points for muscles in the body. Tendons are made of bundles of tissue called sinew that are packed together and twisted like the fibres in a rope. These fibres of sinew are also formed from collagen.

A magnified view of a tendon shows how the fibres are lined up, like the strands in a rope.

Tendons usually cross over joints. When a muscle contracts it pulls on the tendon, moving the bone on the other side of the joint. If you look at the back of your hand as you wriggle your fingers you should be able to see the tendons move beneath the skin as they tug on your fingers, pulled by muscles in your forearm.

Achilles tendon

The Achilles tendon, running from the calf muscle to the heel, is the strongest and thickest tendon in the body. When the calf muscle contracts, it pulls on the Achilles tendon, which pushes the foot downwards. Walking, running, jumping and standing on tiptoe all involve tugging on the Achilles tendon. With every step, it is pulled with a force equivalent to your entire body weight. During a sprint race the pull on the Achilles tendon can be the equivalent of three to twelve times a person's body weight.

▶ *A network of ligaments and tendons gives the foot great flexibility and strength.*

Ligament _____

Ligament _____

Tendon _____

Achilles tendon

Heel bone

Over 600 muscles in your body keep everything on the move. Together they make up half of your body's weight. From walking upstairs, to writing your name and keeping the blood flowing around your body – none of it would happen without muscles. There are three types of muscle tissue: smooth muscle, cardiac muscle and striated, or skeletal, muscle.

Striated muscle

The type of muscle that people are most familiar with is called striated, or skeletal muscle. Each muscle is made up of bundles of fibres. It is called striated muscle because under the microscope the fibres form alternate light and dark stripes, or striations. Connective tissue keeps the fibre bundles together.

The fibres consist of very fine myofibres, or muscle cells. These long, thin cells can be up to 30 cm (12 in) long. Each muscle cell contains bundles of hundreds of even smaller fibres called myofibrils. These are in turn made up of narrower parts called myofilaments.

There are two types of myofilaments, both of which are proteins, and they can slide past each other to shorten the muscle tissue. Hold your hands out in front of you and slide the fingers of one hand between the fingers of the other. In simple terms, this is what is

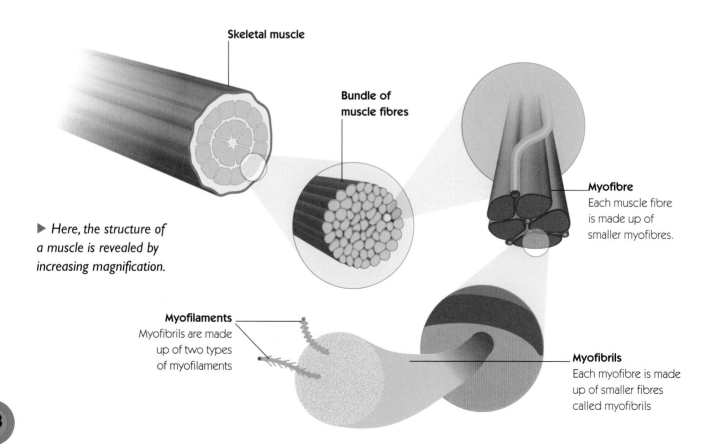

Skeletal muscle

Bundle of muscle fibres

▶ Here, the structure of a muscle is revealed by increasing magnification.

Myofibre
Each muscle fibre is made up of smaller myofibres.

Myofilaments
Myofibrils are made up of two types of myofilaments

Myofibrils
Each myofibre is made up of smaller fibres called myofibrils

Sprinters use fast twitch muscle fibres, which give great power over short periods of time.

happening inside the muscles that you are using to move your hands. It is this movement of millions of tiny protein fibres that causes muscles to contract.

Fast and slow

There are two different types of fibres in striated muscle: slow twitch muscle fibres and fast twitch muscle fibres. Slow twitch muscle fibres contract slowly, but can keep going for a long time. They are good for endurance activities like long distance running.

Fast twitch muscle fibres contract quickly, but they get tired quickly. They are good for quick movements like jumping to catch a ball or running a sprint race. Most of your muscles are made up of both slow and fast twitch muscle fibres.

Body facts

The biggest muscles are the gluteus maximus muscles in the buttocks, each weighing a kilogram (2 lb 3 oz) or more.

The smallest muscle is the 1-mm (0.04-in) long stapedius. It is found inside the ear.

The longest muscle is the sartorius muscle, which runs along the length of the thigh and can reach 50 cm (20 in) in length.

The widest muscle is the external oblique muscle, found in the abdomen. It is 45 cm (17.5 in) across.

Muscular movements

Muscles contract and pull, but they cannot push. So how then can you push something? The answer is that your muscles work together in teams allowing your body to make countless complex movements that you accomplish every day, mostly without you even thinking about it.

Muscle partners

A typical skeletal muscle bulges in the middle and tapers off at the ends, where it is anchored to the skeleton by tendons. When you tense a muscle, it gets shorter and thicker and pulls on whichever other part of the body it is attached to. Many muscles work together in pairs – called antagonistic partners. A muscle on one side of a bone pulls it one way, and the muscle on the other side pulls it back again.

Examples of muscles working in partnership like this include the muscles that bend and straighten your arms and legs. For instance, the biceps muscle on your upper arm pulls your lower arm upwards when it contracts. The triceps muscle at the back of the upper arm pulls the lower arm down when it contracts. So, to bend your arm, the biceps pulls while the triceps relaxes, and to lower it again the biceps relaxes and the triceps pulls.

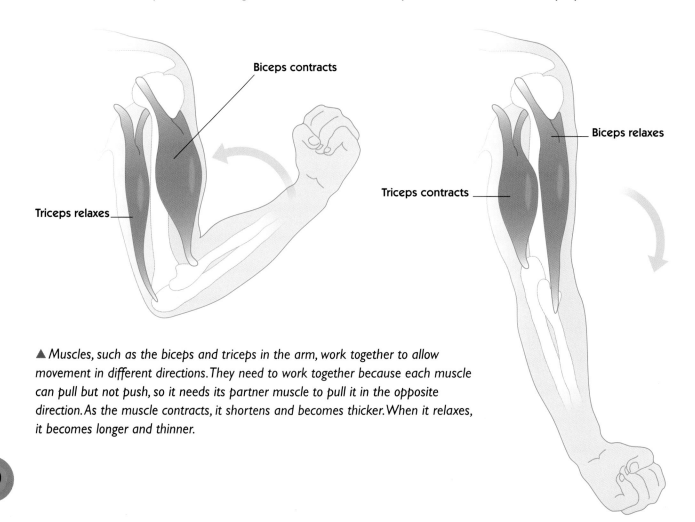

Biceps contracts

Triceps relaxes

Biceps relaxes

Triceps contracts

▲ Muscles, such as the biceps and triceps in the arm, work together to allow movement in different directions. They need to work together because each muscle can pull but not push, so it needs its partner muscle to pull it in the opposite direction. As the muscle contracts, it shortens and becomes thicker. When it relaxes, it becomes longer and thinner.

Living levers

Muscles and bones act like levers. A lever is a simple mechanism that requires a fulcrum, or pivot point, a load and some force. One example of a lever can be found in your forearm. To pick up a cup of tea (the load), you must lift your forearm. Your biceps pulls on the bone in your forearm, providing force. Your elbow acts as the fulcrum.

This type of lever actually works best in giving speed and range of movement rather than lifting power. Although the muscle itself contracts only a centimetre or two, it causes the forearm to move over a much greater distance.

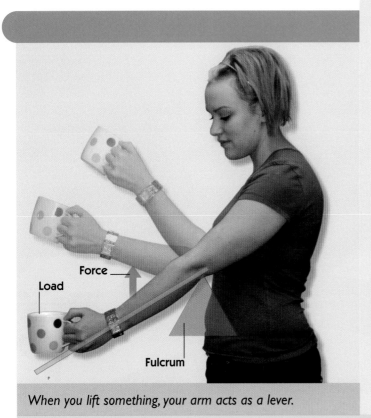

When you lift something, your arm acts as a lever.

Investigate

There are three different types of levers: first-class, second-class and third-class.

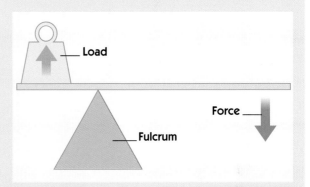

In a first-class lever (above), the fulcrum is between the load and the force. In a second-class lever (below) the load is between the fulcrum and the force.

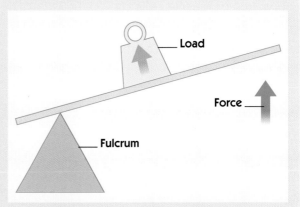

In a third-class lever, such as your forearm (left), the force is between the load and the fulcrum. Can you find examples of these different levers around your home and in your body?

Delicate movements

Our muscles are capable of the most delicate movements. The muscles of the face and hands in particular can be used with enormous control. Just think of the huge range of facial expressions we can all make – each and every one produced by the movements of over 50 small muscles in the face.

Moving muscles

The contraction of a muscle is triggered by a signal from a nerve fibre that links to the muscle fibres. For example, when you decide to kick a ball, signals travel from your brain, along your spinal cord and out to the nerves leading to your leg muscles. In a large muscle, one nerve fibre can send a signal that causes thousands of muscle cells to contract at the same time – ideal if you want to give a ball a good hard kick.

Precision movement

What happens if you want to do something that requires more control than kicking? In the smaller muscles that move the fingers or swivel the eyeball, each nerve fibre may trigger only a dozen or so muscle fibres, allowing great precision in movement.

Each eyeball is controlled by six muscles that are fixed to different points around the

When you smile, you use 15 different muscles in your face.

side of the eyeball. Each one can contract and relax with great precision and is capable of extremely subtle control. They can move the eyeball by as little as a tenth of a millimetre (0.004 in) at a time.

Muscles and speech

Talking requires the use of many different muscles, some of which are used with great control. The chest muscles we use for breathing supply a flow of air from the lungs. We use muscles in the larynx, or voice box, to produce subtle changes in pitch as the air from the lungs passes through. Stretching the larynx by just 2 mm (0.08 in) will produce a high-pitched shriek. Another complex set of muscles shapes the mouth and moves the tongue to produce the sounds of speech.

Body facts

Some artists show astonishing muscle control of the eye and hand. Figures can be carved from objects such as a single grain of rice using tiny blades of diamond. Artist Willard Wigan paints his creations using a single hair plucked from a dead fly. He has carved a tiny Statue of Liberty that fits inside the eye of a needle and a boxing ring, complete with boxers, that is smaller than the head of a matchstick.

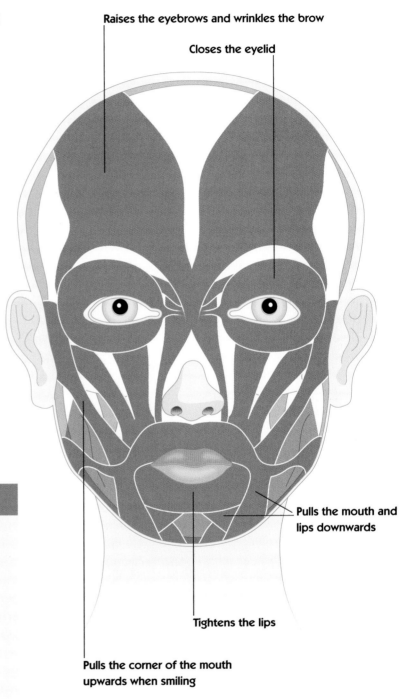

Raises the eyebrows and wrinkles the brow

Closes the eyelid

Pulls the mouth and lips downwards

Tightens the lips

Pulls the corner of the mouth upwards when smiling

▲ This diagram shows how the face muscles are arranged and what some of them do. This network of muscles can be used with great control and subtlety, enabling us to make a huge range of facial expressions. We also use these muscles to eat, talk and blink.

Smooth muscle

Smooth muscle is so-called because, unlike striated muscle, it does not have a striped appearance when looked at under a microscope. It is also called involuntary muscle because it contracts and relaxes automatically without our conscious control. For example, smooth muscle keeps everything moving through your digestive system.

Sacs and tubes

Smooth muscle is not attached to bone but generally forms tubes or sacs. It forms the digestive system and lines blood vessels, the bladder and the airways. In women it also forms the uterus (womb).

Smooth muscle lining blood vessels adjusts the flow of blood through those vessels by making them narrower or wider. In this way, blood pressure and the supply of blood to different parts of the body is controlled. Ring-shaped sphincter muscles made of

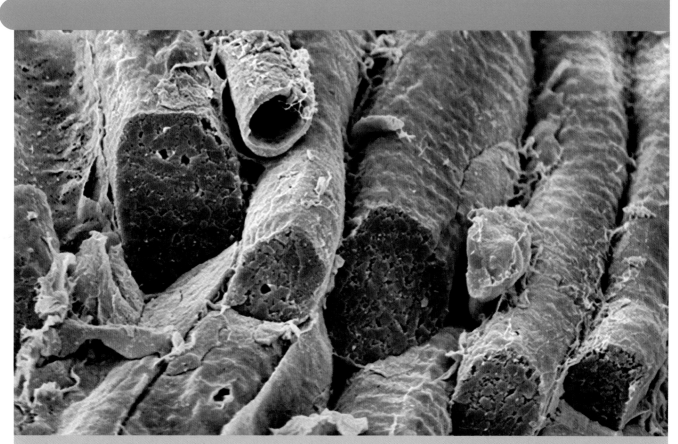

This magnified image shows smooth muscle fibres, such as those found in the digestive system. The pink tube at the top is a blood vessel.

Smooth muscle automatically opens and closes the eye's pupil in response to changing light levels.

smooth muscle tissue control entry from one part of the digestive system to another, for example from the stomach to the small intestine. Smooth muscle is also responsible for movements, such as the closing of the eye's pupil in bright light.

Muscle layers

The fibres of smooth muscle are arranged in layers that contract in different directions. For example, circular muscle fibres around the intestine make it longer and thinner, while lengthways muscle fibres make it shorter and fatter. The alternating movements of these two types of smooth muscle move food along in the wave-like motion called peristalsis.

Smooth muscle cells are small compared to skeletal muscle cells and are generally spindle shaped. When a smooth muscle cell contracts, it pulls in all directions, rather than shortening along its length like a skeletal muscle cell. Not all of the fibres in smooth muscle tissue

contract at the same time; instead the fibres work in relays. While some are contracted, others relax and recover before they contract in their turn. In this way, the smooth muscle can work continuously without tiring.

Body facts

The airways in your lungs are opened and closed by smooth muscle. In some people, an allergic reaction to something such as dust, pollen or animals can inflame the airways, causing this muscle to contract suddenly and making it difficult to breathe. This breathing problem is called asthma. Sufferers have to use drugs, which are squirted into the mouth using a special aerosol spray. The drugs then act on the contracted smooth muscle in the airways, causing them to relax again.

Cardiac muscle

On average your heart will beat around a 100 times a minute, every minute, every day, right the way through your life. If you want to get some idea of how much work the heart does, try squeezing a tennis ball 100 times in a minute. The chances are your hand might be feeling a little tired at the end of it. Could you do it for another minute? This is roughly what your heart is doing all the time.

Heart muscle

The heart is made of a type of muscle that is not found anywhere else in the body. It is like a combination of skeletal muscle and smooth muscle. Looked at under a microscope, heart muscle has the striped fibres of skeletal muscle, but the fibres branch off in different directions like smooth muscle. It is this branching of the fibres, or muscle cells, that makes them squeeze the heart in when they contract.

If they all pointed in the same direction, they would only pull in that one direction. The heart cells are linked to each other in a way that allows signals to spread rapidly from one cell to another, so that they all contract together.

Heart maintenance

Unlike other muscles in your body, cardiac muscle never gets tired. One of the reasons for this is that heart muscle cells are held

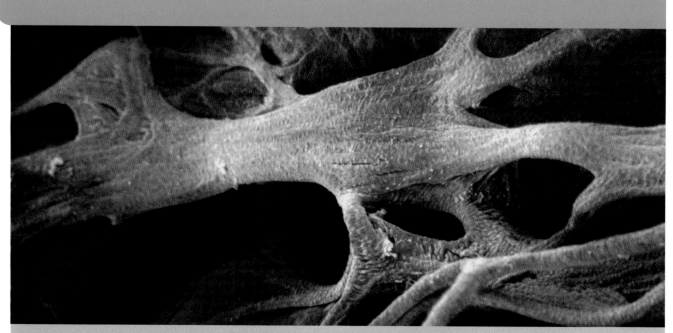

Some of the heart's specialised 'pacemaker' cells are shown here in green. These produce the electrical impulses that trigger each heartbeat.

within a type of connective tissue that is rich in blood vessels. The blood supply to the heart brings it all the oxygen and glucose it needs and rapidly removes the wastes that cause other muscles to tire.

Electrical signals

You never have to think about making your heart contract. A small patch of cells generates pulses of electrical signals. These signals are carried to the muscle fibres in the walls of the heart's ventricles, making them contract. The heart's 'wiring system' is set up so that the wave of contractions begins at the base of the heart. This means that blood is pumped up and out through the main arteries and doesn't collect in the base of the heart.

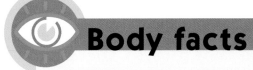

The average human heart measures 12 cm by 9 cm (5 by 3.5 in) and weighs between 250 and 390 grams (8.8 – 13.8 ounces).

Your heart beats over a 100,000 times a day, over 36 million times a year and more than 2.5 billion times in the course of an average lifespan.

The heart pumps 7,500 litres (1,980 gallons) of blood around the body every day.

The heart produces enough pressure to squirt blood 10 m (33 ft).

Stages in a heartbeat

▼ *The right and left atria fill with blood. Blue areas indicate blood that is low in oxygen, while red areas indicate blood that is high in oxygen.*

▼ *The right and left atria contract to squeeze blood into the ventricles.*

▼ *The ventricles contract, forcing blood into the arteries. Blood low in oxygen goes into the pulmonary artery and on to the lungs, while blood high in oxygen moves into the aorta and on to the rest of the body.*

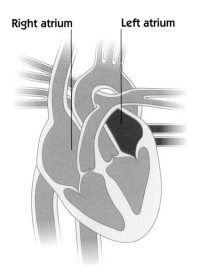

Right atrium   Left atrium

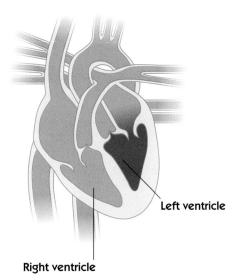

Right ventricle

Left ventricle

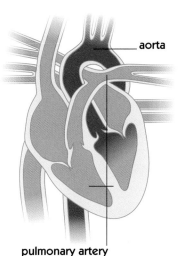

aorta

pulmonary artery

Muscular disorders

Disorders of the muscles can be painful and, in the worst cases, they may even cause paralysis. Over the course of your life your muscles do a lot of work, so it should come as no surprise that sometimes things go wrong. Perhaps the amazing thing is that things don't go wrong more often.

Sprains and strains

Muscle disorders such as sprains and strains can be the result of injury or overuse. A sprain is caused by a stretched or torn ligament. Falling awkwardly or getting hit, for example by a fast-moving ball, can cause a sprain. Sprained ankles and wrists are common injuries that result in pain, swelling, bruising and being unable to move the joint.

A strain is caused by a stretched, or torn, muscle or tendon. Strains can happen suddenly or they may develop over time. Many people get strains playing sports, resulting in pain, muscle spasms, swelling and difficulty moving the muscle.

Treating sprains and strains involves resting the injured part, perhaps for as long as 48 hours, before weight is put on it. If possible, put ice on the injury as this will help to reduce swelling. The area should be bandaged up to prevent movement, and it is a good idea to keep the injured part of the body elevated if possible.

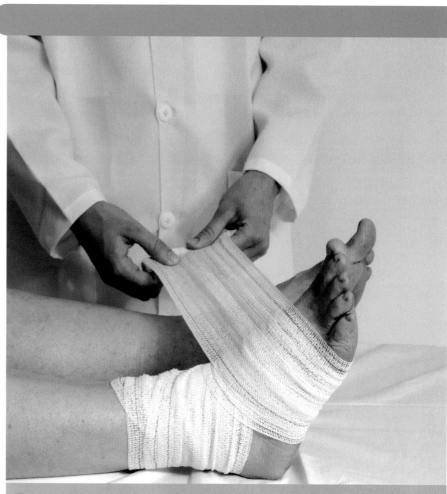

Treating a sprain involves immobilising the joint to prevent movement that might cause further damage.

Athletes who put a great deal of strain on their muscles may sometimes suffer from painful cramps.

muscles. They can be treated by gently massaging and stretching the affected muscle.

Muscular dystrophy

More serious muscle disorders include muscular dystrophy (MD), a genetic illness that causes muscle weakness and muscle loss. Some forms of MD appear in infancy, while others may not appear until middle age or later. All forms of MD grow worse as the person's muscles get weaker. Most people with MD eventually lose the ability to walk. As yet, there is no cure for this condition.

Neuromuscular disorders

Some conditions don't affect the muscles directly but cause problems with the nerves that control the muscles. These are called neuromuscular disorders. One such disorder is multiple sclerosis (MS). The nerves become damaged, blocking signals between the brain and the rest of the body, with the result that it becomes difficult to control the muscles. Some people lose the ability to speak or walk.

In 2008, researchers had great hopes that they had found a drug that would halt the progress of MS. There is no doubt that the work will continue until a cure is found.

Cramps

Muscle cramps are sudden, painful contractions in one or more of your muscles. They often occur after exercise or at night, and can last a few seconds or for several minutes. There are several causes of muscle cramps. They can be caused by malfunctioning nerves or by straining or overusing a muscle. Cramps may also be caused by dehydration, by a lack of minerals in the diet or by insufficient blood getting to the

Fun facts

Big bones
The largest dinosaur that has been discovered is the Argentinosaurus, a monster herbivore. It stood over 20 m (65 ft) tall, was over 36 m (118 ft) long and weighed up to 90 tonnes (100 tons). Each of its immense vertebrae were 1.5 m (5 ft) long and 1.5 m (5 ft) wide.

Decorating with bones
The Sedlec Ossuary is a small chapel in the town of Kutna Hora in the Czech Republic. It is decorated with the bones of between 40,000 and 70,000 human skeletons, many dating back to the 14th century.

This chandelier is in the chapel at Kutna Hora in the Czech Republic. It contains every bone that can be found in the human body!

Spineless species
No one really knows how many different species of animal there are on the Earth. There may be 50 million or more. We do know that the animals without skeletons hugely outnumber the animals with skeletons. More than 97 per cent of animals are classed as invertebrates – animals without backbones – and the vast majority of them are insects.

Revealing x-rays
Until Wilhelm Roentgen discovered x-rays at the end of the nineteenth century, there was no way to see inside the body without surgery. The first x-ray photograph was taken in 1895. It was of Roentgen's wife's hand and clearly showed the bones inside. Roentgen's discovery brought about a revolution in medicine.

Strong bones
The adult human femur (thigh bone) can support a load of around 900 kilograms (1,980 lbs), or more than ten times the weight of the average adult male.

Musical bones
The oldest known musical instruments are flutes carved from animal bone. Examples have been discovered in France that are more than 35,000 years old.

At home in the bones
Some of the oldest homes made by humans were built using mammoth bones. They were built around 25,000 years ago in Southern Moravia, a region of the Czech Republic.

The speed of a mantis shrimp's strike is similar to that of a bullet fired from a rifle.

Giant jawbone

The biggest jawbone belongs to the sperm whale. This bone can measure up to 5 m (16 ft) long.

Keeping an eye on things

You use your eye muscles more than any other muscle in your body. You consciously move your eyes more than 100,000 times every day.

Mighty muscles

The official world record in the +105 kg +233 lbs) weightlifting class is held by Hossein Rezazadeh of Iran, who lifted 263.5 kg (581 lbs) at the 2004 Olympic Games.

Slow heartbeat

The mammal with the slowest heartbeat is the giant blue whale – its 450-kg (995-lb) heart beats just four to eight times a minute.

Shattering shrimps

Mantis shrimps can deliver blows with their hammer-like claws that can break the glass in an aquarium tank. They use their striking power to shatter the shells of the snails they hunt. The shrimp locks its claw in position so it can't move and then contracts the muscle, storing energy. When the shrimp strikes, it releases the claw and the stored up energy in a 23-m (75-ft) per second flash.

Muscle-powered micromachine

In 2004, scientists at the University of California succeeded in making a tiny robot that was powered by rat heart muscle cells. As the muscle cells contract and relax the microrobot 'walks' along. One day the technology might be used to create muscle-powered micromachines that repair holes in spacecraft.

Activities

Get Moving!

Everyone agrees that exercise is good for you, but different types of exercise can be good for you in different ways. To keep fit and healthy, try to do some of each of the following types of exercise on a regular basis.

Muscle strengtheners Doing sit-ups and press-ups, going for a run, riding your bike and swimming will all help to keep your muscles in shape. With stronger muscles you'll find it easier to do all kinds of things.

Flexibility exercise Most children are more flexible than most adults – why not keep it that way? Do some bending and stretching, try some yoga or dancing or take up a martial art. You will be amazed by what your body can do.

Aerobic exercise Your heart is a muscle, so give it some exercise. Aerobic exercises are best for your heart. Aerobic means 'with air' and in aerobic exercise you breathe faster than normal, supplying your muscles with the oxygen they need. Aerobic exercises get your heart pumping and make it better at its job of shifting oxygen-carrying blood cells around the body. Run fast, push those bike pedals round, get your skates on, and get that heart working!

More reasons to exercise

In addition to strengthening muscles, helping you stay flexible and keeping your heart healthy, exercise also benefits you in the following ways:

Exercise helps to build up your bone mass. This strengthens the bones so they can deal with the extra stresses and strains of exercising. Strengthening your bones will benefit you in later life when your bone mass begins to decrease, lessening the chance of having fragile, easily broken bones.

It helps to keep you in shape. Your body needs energy and it gets that energy from the food you eat. If you take in more energy than you need – in other words if you eat too much – the body stores some of the extra energy as fat. The more you exercise, the more energy you'll need. Exercising gives you a good appetite and builds your muscles – not your fat reserves!

You'll feel great. If your body is strong and flexible and your heart is healthy it will help you to be confident about yourself and to have fun doing things.

Martial arts can help in building strength and flexibility.

Clench test

Hold your hand up above your head and clench and unclench your fist. Count how many times you can do it before it starts to ache. Then try the same thing with your other hand down by your side. You should be able to do more clenches with your hand down by your side. This is because it is easier for blood to flow down to the muscles in your hand than it is to flow up to them.

Test your bone knowledge

1) How many bones are there in the adult human body?

2) What is the name of the only bone in your body not connected to any other bone by a joint and where would you find it?

3) Where are the saddle joints found?

4) Which is the longest bone in your body?

5) What is the name for the tissues that connect muscles to bones?

6) Your bones become fully developed at about what age?

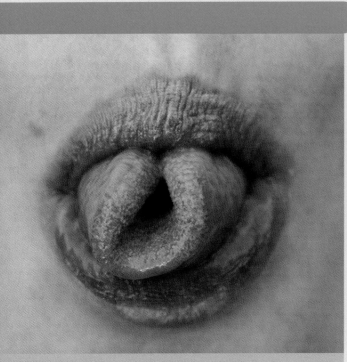

Will your tongue muscles let you do this? Not everyone can!

Let's talk exercise!

When you speak, you use muscles in your tongue, lips, jaw and vocal cords. Some of these muscles can benefit from exercise, too. Try some of these tongue twisters to get them working. Tongue twisters are phrases that are difficult to say over and over. Repeat the following phrases as fast as you can.

• Unique New York
• Red lorry, yellow lorry
• A box of biscuits, a batch of mixed biscuits
• Six thick thistle sticks
• Toy boat
• Sam's shop stocks short spotted socks
• Round the rugged rocks the ragged rascals ran.

Answers
1 206
2 The hyoid bone in the neck
3 In your thumbs
4 The femur, or thigh bone
5 Tendons
6 At about age 20

43

Glossary

allergic to do with allergies, the body's reaction against materials like pollen or dust that cause irritation

appendicular skeleton the part of the skeleton that includes the bones of the limbs and pelvis

axial skeleton the part of the skeleton that includes the skull, spinal column, ribs and sternum

carpal bones the eight bones that together make up the wrist

cells the smallest things that may be classed as living; some living things, such as bacteria, are single-celled organisms; others, such as humans, are multi-celled organisms made up of trillions of cells working together

chondroblast a type of cell that forms cartilage cells

collagen a type of protein that is one of the major components of tissues such as tendons and skin

femur the thigh bone

fibroblast a type of cell that makes collagen and other parts of connective tissue

fibula the outer, smaller bone of the lower leg

foetus a baby in the womb, from eight weeks after conception until birth

genes the basic units of inheritance, the characteristics passed from parent to child

haematoma a mass of clotted blood that forms where blood vessels have been broken

hormone a chemical messenger produced in one part of the body and carried in the bloodstream to trigger a reaction in another part of the body

lamellae concentric layers of bone

menopause the time when a woman's menstrual cycle ceases and she can no longer have children

minerals simple chemicals that are needed by the body in small amounts to allow it to function properly

ossification the process of bone formation

osteoblasts specialised cells that form new bone

osteocytes osteoblasts that have completed their bone-forming function and are held within the bone helping to maintain it

osteon a ring of osteocytes embedded around a central canal; the basic unit of bone

paralysis the loss of the ability to move a part of the body

periosteum the layer of connective tissue that covers a bone

phalanges the 14 bones that make up the fingers of a hand

protein a group of complex molecules produced by living things to perform a variety of tasks in the body, including building cell structures

sinew a tough band of connective tissue joining muscle to bone

skeletal to do with the skeleton

sphincter a circular band of muscle that opens and closes a passageway in the body

stamina the strength and energy to do something over a long period

sternum the flat, narrow bone in the centre of the chest

synovial fluid a clear fluid that lubricates joints in the body

tarsal bones the seven bones that make up the ankle

tibia the shin bone, the larger of the two bones in the lower leg

tissues groups of similar cells in the body, such as muscle tissue or nerve tissue

vertebrae the 22 bones that make up the spine

vitamins a group of essential compounds that are involved in a variety of processes in the body and are needed in small amounts in the diet for good health

Further information

Body Science: The Human Skeleton,
Richard Walker,
Franklin Watts, 2007

Our Bodies: Muscles and the Skeleton,
Steve Parker,
Wayland, 2006

My Healthy Body: Skeleton,
Jen Green,
Franklin Watts, 2008

My Healthy Body: Muscles,
Jen Green,
Franklin Watts, 2008

Websites
http://kidshealth.org/kid/htbw/bones.html
A straightforward guide to bones and taking care of them.

http://www.aboutkidshealth.ca/HowTheBodyWorks/Skeleton.aspx?articleID=10093&categoryID=XT
A good illustrated guide to the skeleton and the anatomy of the bones and joints that make it up.

http://www.bbc.co.uk/science/humanbody/body/factfiles/muscle_anatomy.shtml
Introduction to the major muscle groups with animations showing them in action.

Index